THE SCHREIBERS

The Apple Doesn't
Fall Far From the Tree

Maxine Schreiber

THE SCHREIBERS

The Apple Doesn't Fall Far From The Tree

Second Edition

Dedicated to Janet Schreiber without whose support this book would not be possible and to Herman and Anne K. Schreiber, who are smiling down from Heaven. With special thanks to artists David Willison and Chris Oakes who helped me during the process of the original publication in 2011.

ISBN-13: 978-1499115017

ISBN-10: 1499115016

Printed by CreateSpace, An Amazon.com Company

Published by Schreiber Studio
maxine@schreiberstudio.com
www.schreiberstudio.com

Contents

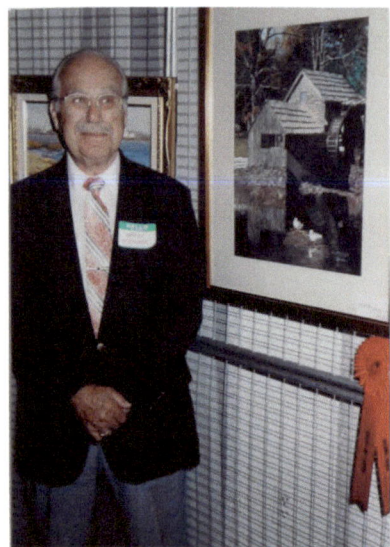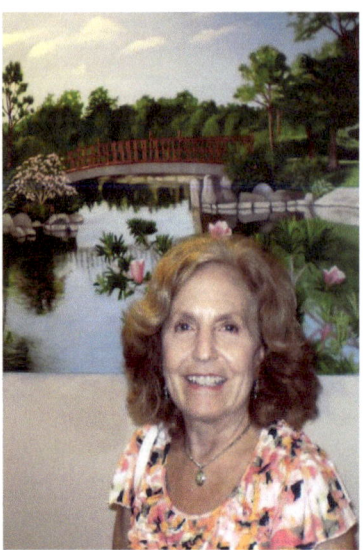

Dad at a Delray Art League exhibit with a Second Place for his Old Mill pastel and me in front of my painting Morikami Bridge at the Coral Springs Museum in 2011.

THE TREE

Art has been an important part of my life as far back as I can remember. My dad, Herman Schreiber, was a master artist, a true "Renaissance man." To support our family, he worked as a jeweler, a trumpet player, an optician, and a tax accountant. But he was always a visual artist, and his creative ability and temperament were a major influence on me. When I was young, we spent hours looking through his treasured book **World Famous Paintings,** and he taught me how to draw.

In the fall of 2011, I was invited to do two Father/Daughter exhibits, mid-November through mid-February in the J. Turner Moore Memorial Library of Manalapan, Florida and the other December through January 31, 2012 in the Student Resource Building of Florida Atlantic

University in Jupiter. Putting the exhibits together inspired this book, a compilation of our works in both shows.

Born in Newark, New Jersey, Dad graduated in 1934 from the Newark School of Fine and Industrial Arts. Though fine art was his first love, after graduating, he chose to play his trumpet to earn a living. Through the years he worked in a number of careers, and occasional sketching was his only art endeavor. It wasn't until he reached his sixties that he resumed painting after receiving a retirement gift of watercolors and pastels from my sister and me. The watercolors dried up, but he never stopped using the pastels.

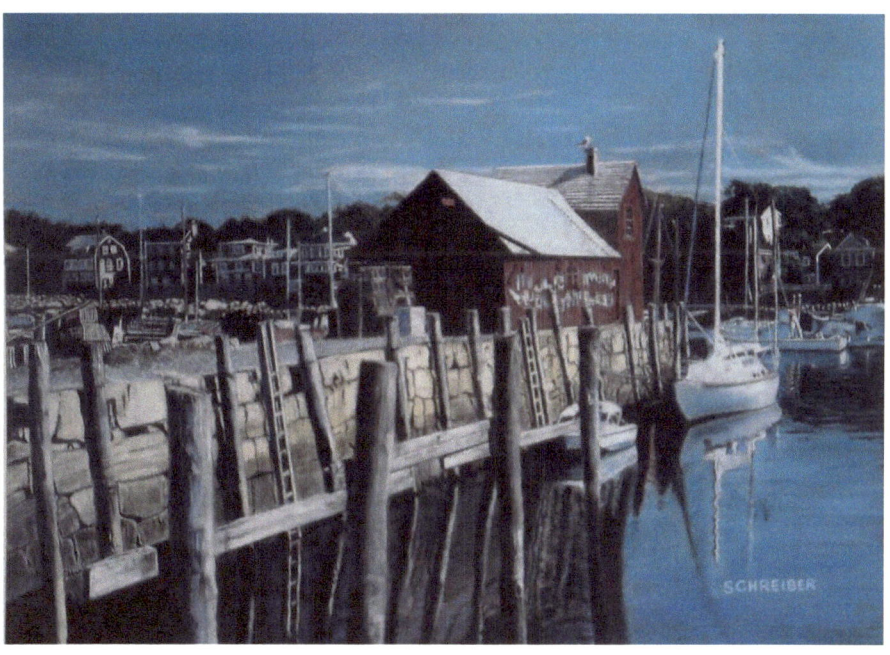

Rockport, 16" x 22" pastel by Herman Schreiber

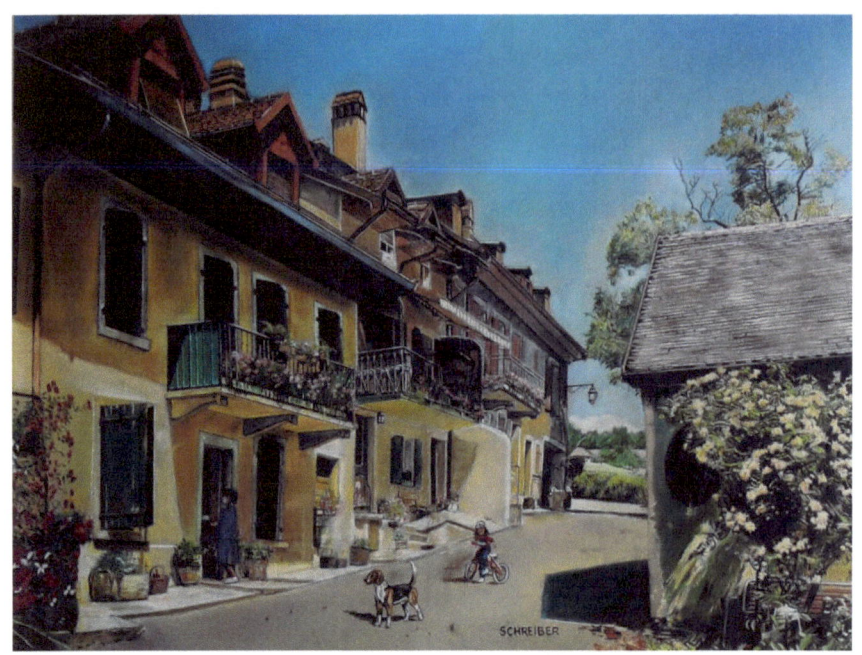

Alpine Village, 18" x 24" pastel by Herman Schreiber

During his late life art career, Herman exhibited his work in galleries and museums in New Jersey where he won many awards including Blue Ribbons at the South Orange Annual Art Show, Bloomfield College, & Montclair State College exhibits.

In Florida 1988 to 1995, as a member of the Delray Art League he exhibited in shows at Old School Square and other Delray sites and won numerous awards. In 1994 & 1995 his work was in the 55th & 56th Annual Juried Exhibitions at the Society of the Four Arts in Palm Beach.

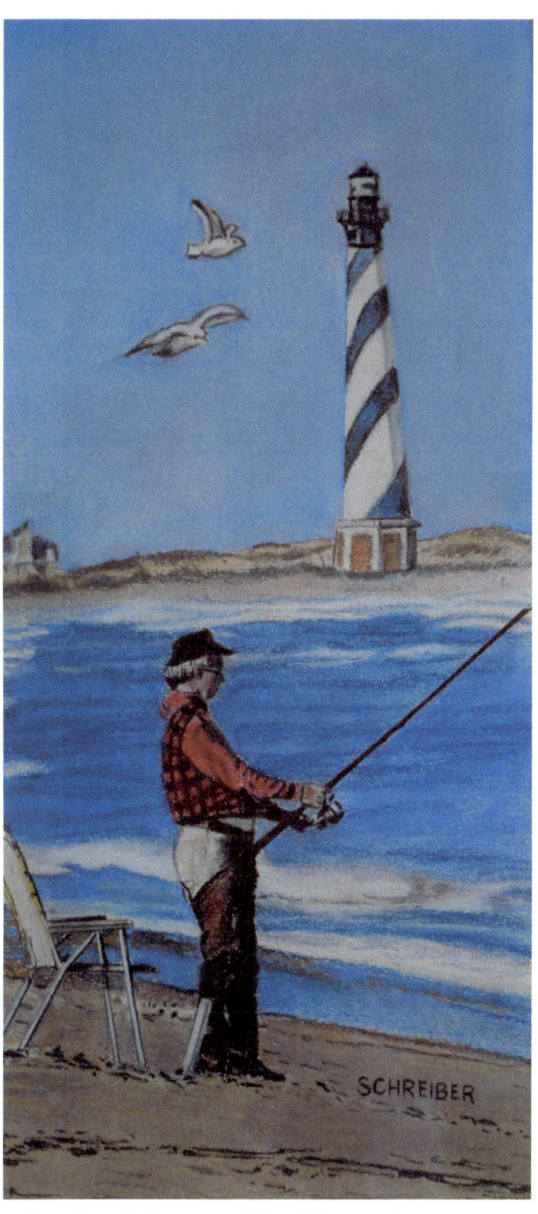
Carolina Fisherman, 6" x 16" pastel

In 1993, he said, "I'm 79 years old and have a back-log of requests to last me until I'm 120. I take my time and work at my own pace. If I had deadlines to worry about, I wouldn't enjoy it. After all, I'm retired. I'm not working for a living. I had to give up playing the trumpet. My front teeth and lips gave out, but my hands are steady, my imagi-nation is vivid, and I enjoy painting."

Dad's life ended on May 8, 1995. Though he's gone, his work lives on bringing pleasure to all who view it.

THE ART OF PASTEL PAINTING

Pastels are dry chalks made of pigment and a weak, non-waxy binder that serves to hold the pigment particles together in the form of a chalk stick. These sticks come in several degrees of hardness, from soft to medium hard. They can be applied with a sharp point or broadly with the side of the pastel stick and rubbed in with the fingers.

In prehistoric periods, images were made on walls of caves with natural chalks and clay. Pastel technique as it is known today was practiced in the middle of the seventeenth century by portrait artists like Robert Nanteuil (1625-78) and in the eighteenth century by Maurice Quentin de la Tour (1704-88). Its use was continued through the nineteenth century by Manet, Degas, and Renoir, and in the twentieth century by Picasso, Redon, and Chagall.

Since pastels are applied in the form of dry chalk, colors remain very much the same as in the pigments from which they are made. Pastels are as lasting as painting of any medium and keep the range and clear intensity of the original pigments much more than does oil or encaustic technique.

Herman Schreiber
"Realistic Portrayals in Pastels"

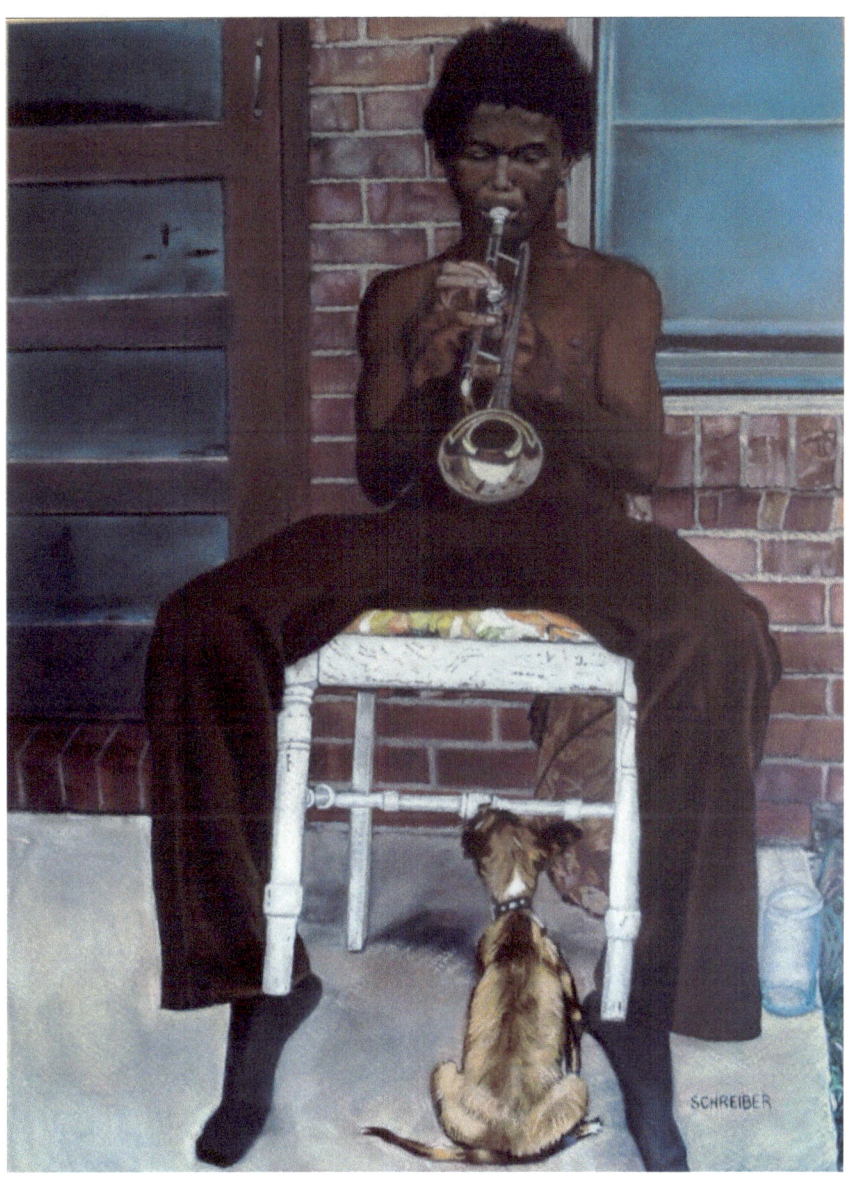

Audience of One, 16" x 23" pastel

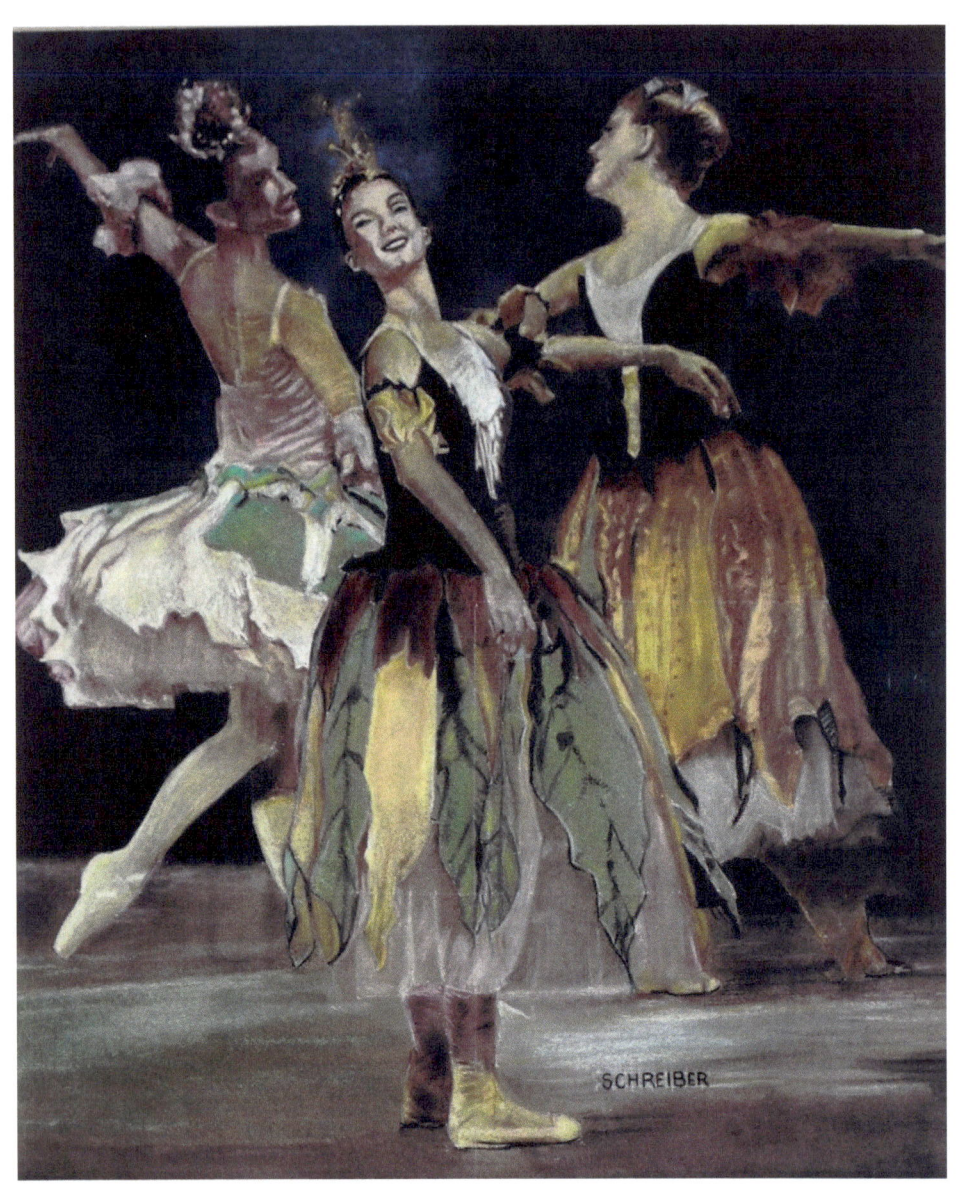

Ballerinas, 20" x 24" pastel

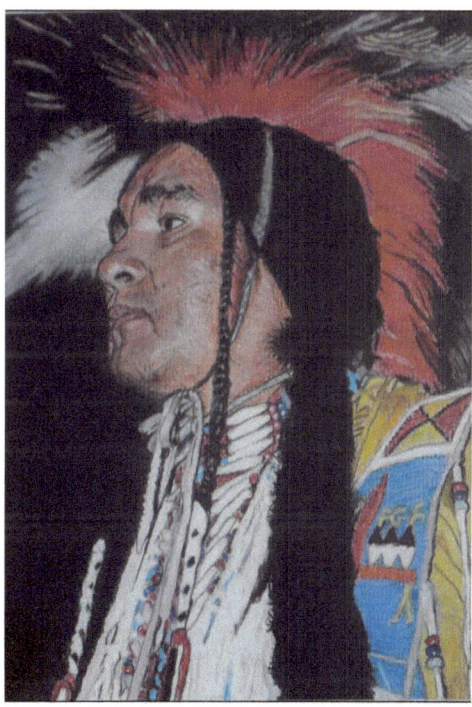

The Indian, 7" x 10"
pastel

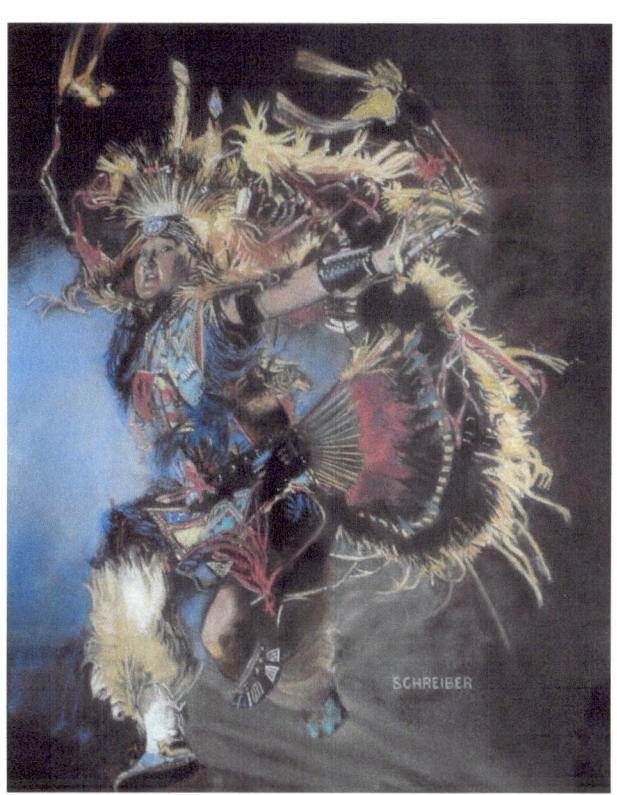

Plains Indian,
16" x 20" pastel

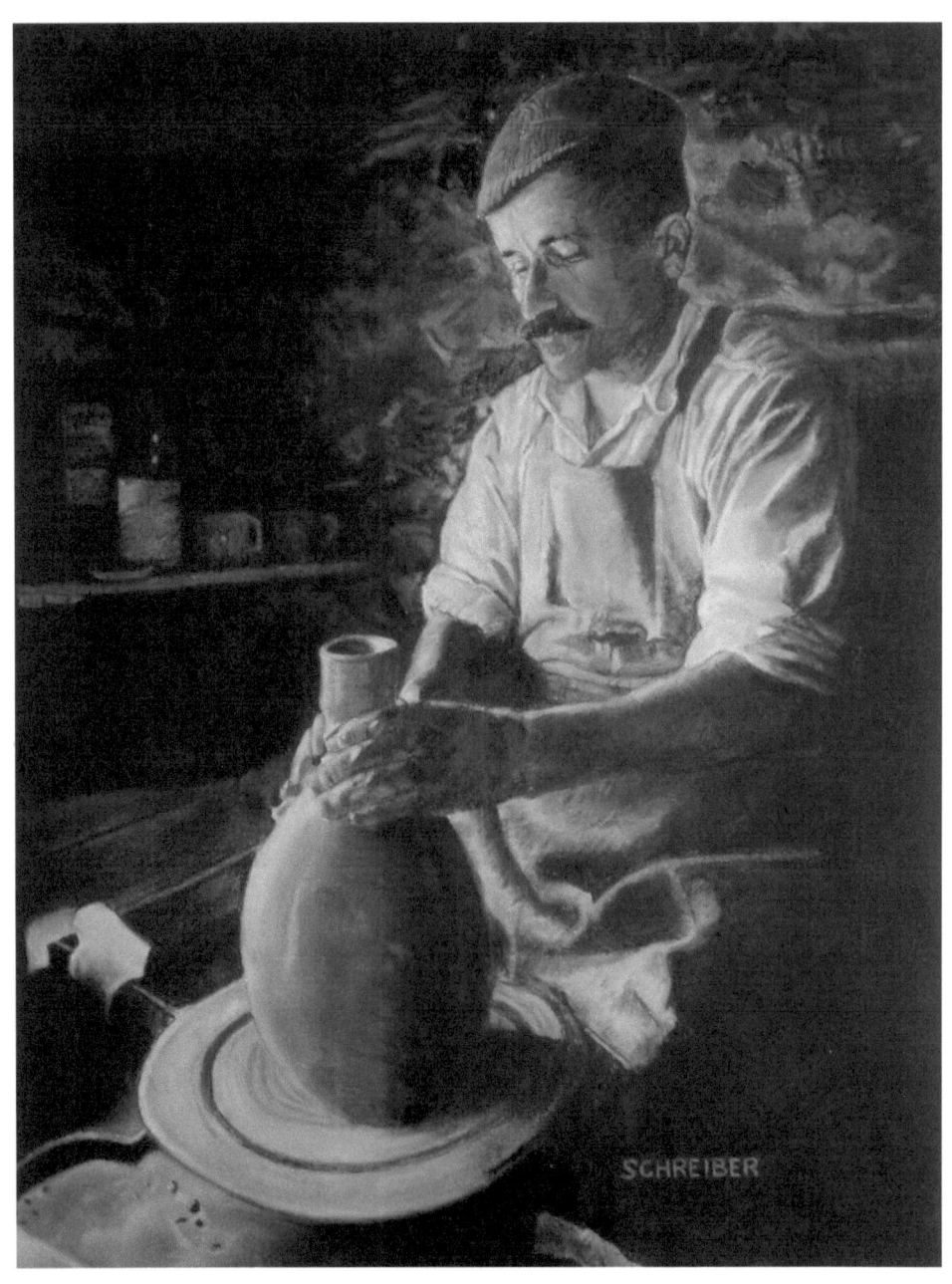

The Potter, 15" x 19" pastel

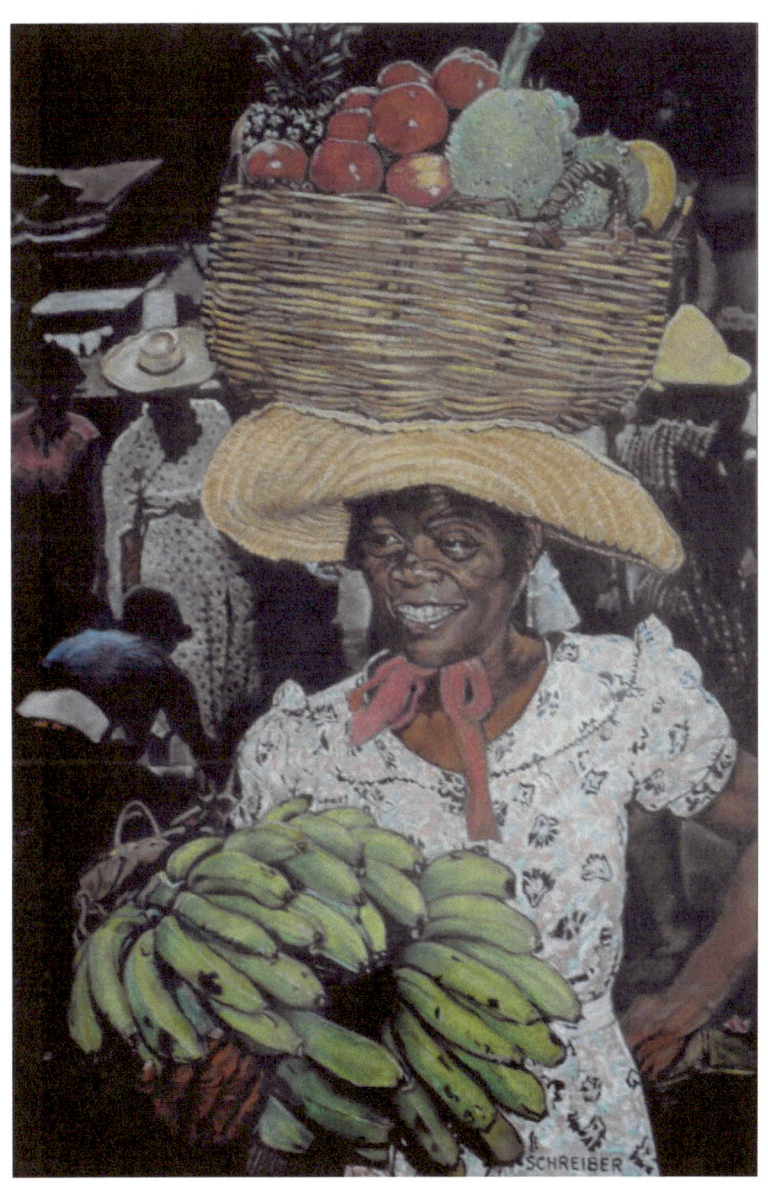

The Fruit Lady, 19" x 25" pastel

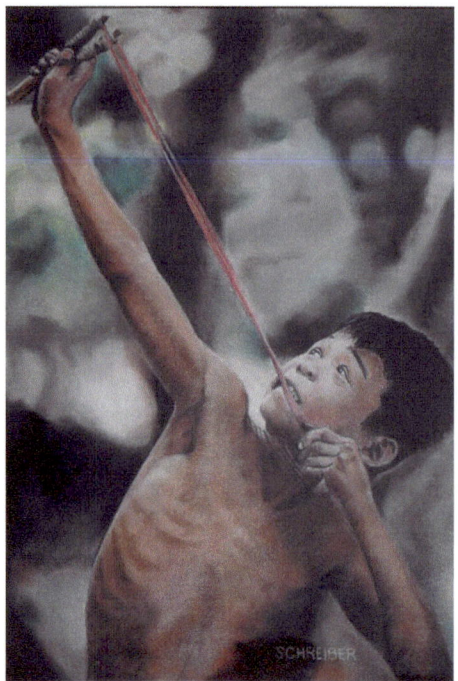

Boy with a Slingshot,
13" x 19" pastel

Girl with Corn Braids
13" x 19" pastel

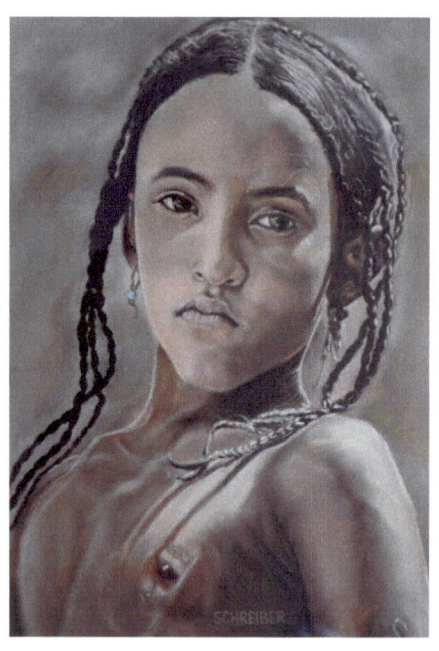

14

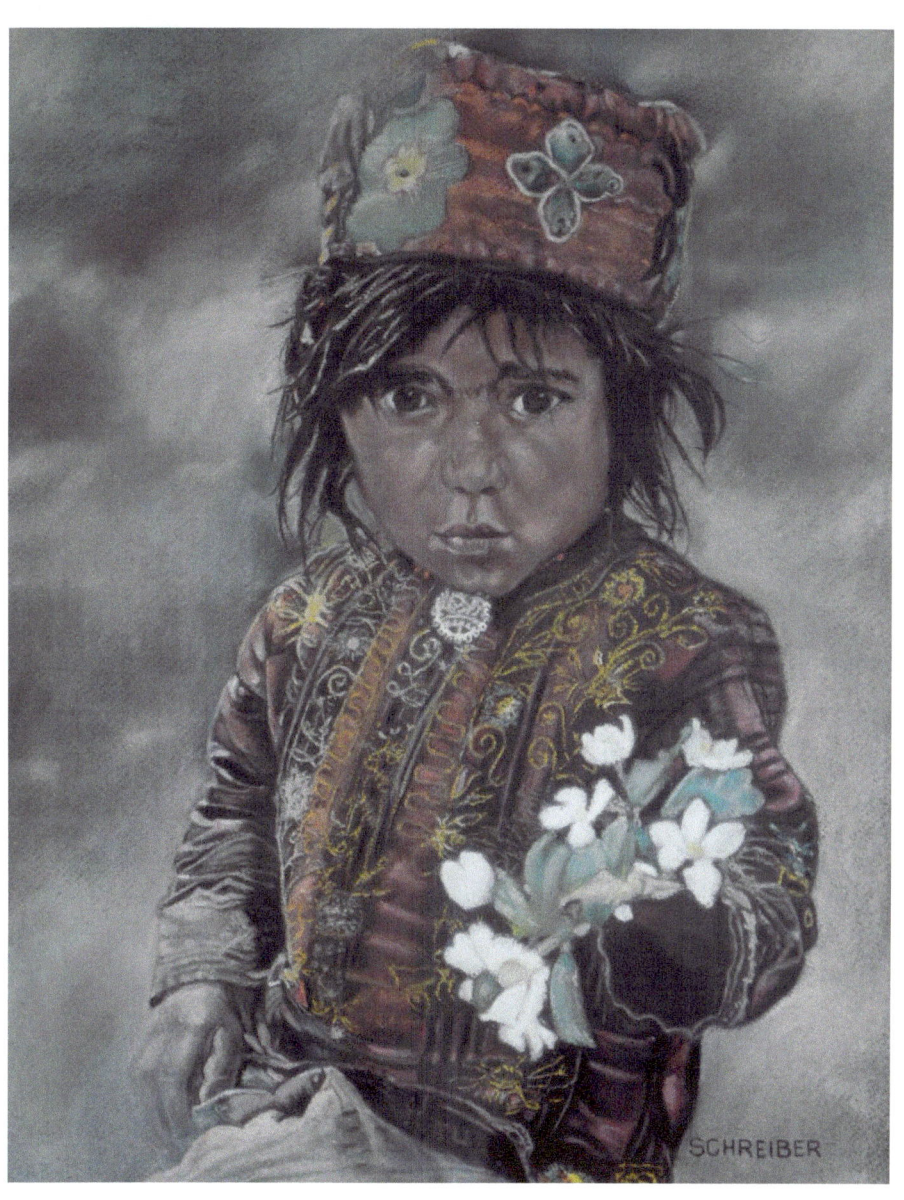

Sima with her Flowers, 14" x 18" pastel

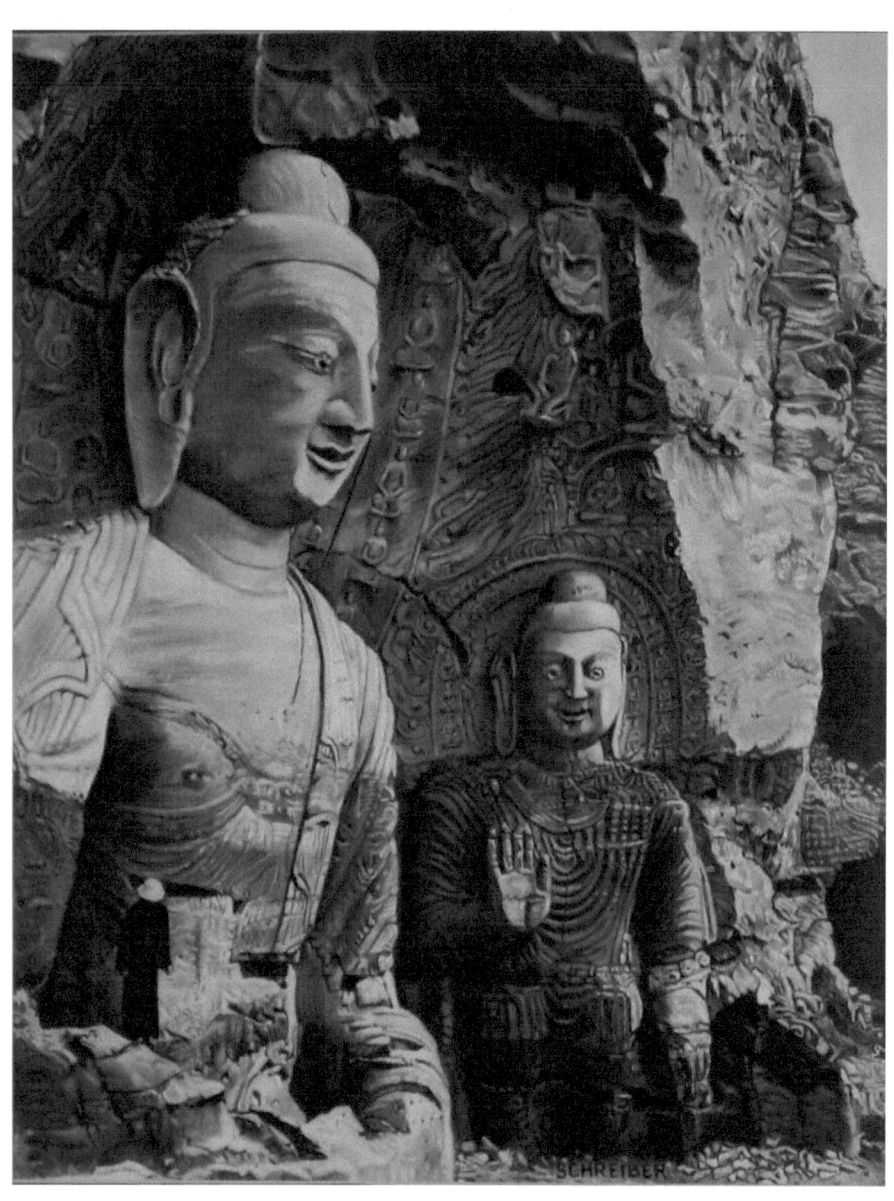

Two Buddhas, 16" x 20" pastel

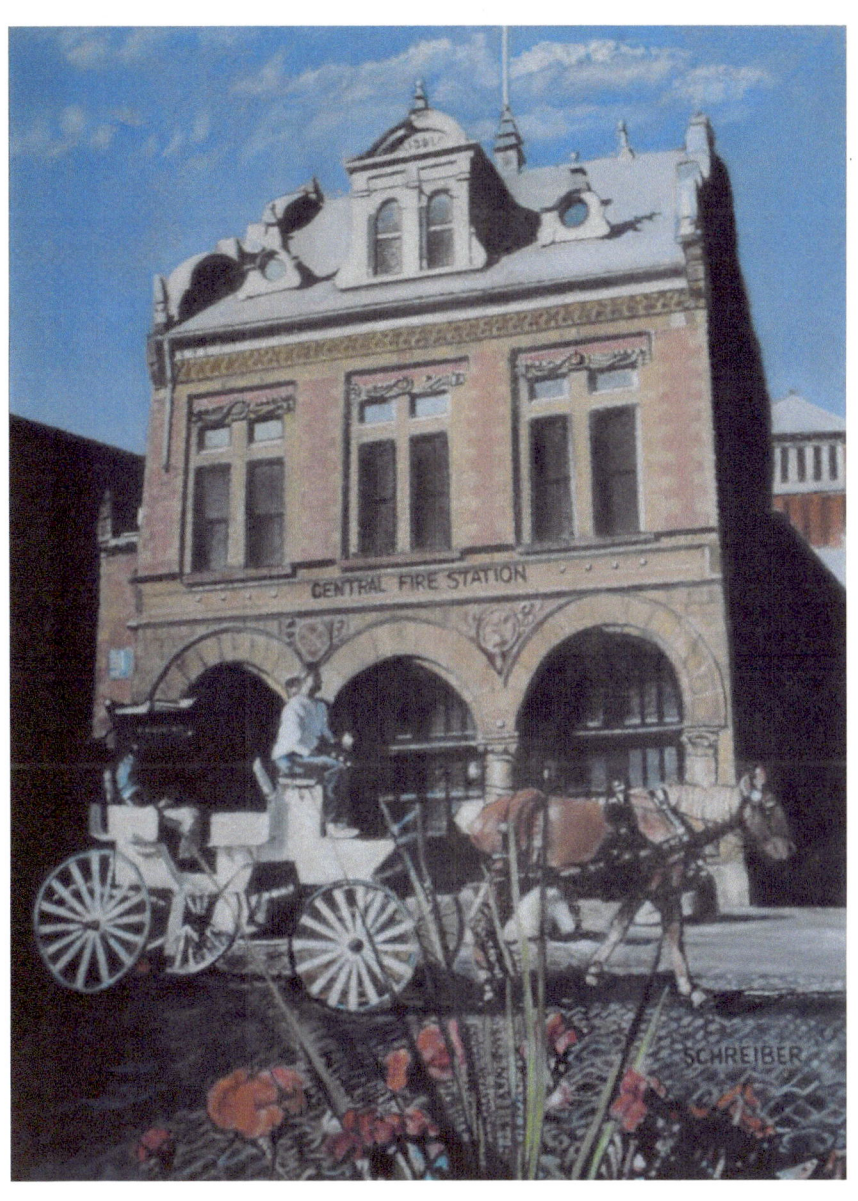

Central Fire Station, 14" x 19" pastel

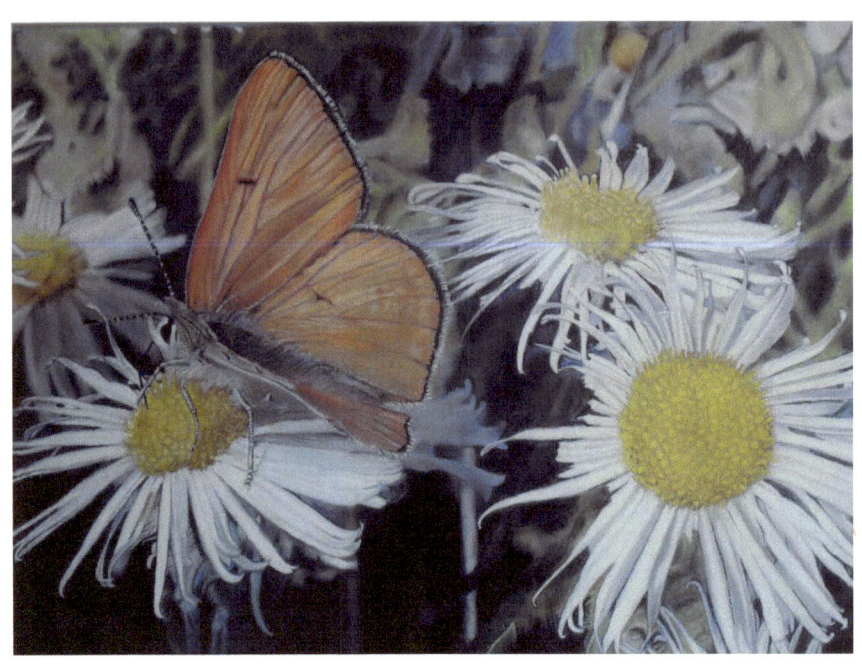

The Butterfly, 17" x 23" pastel

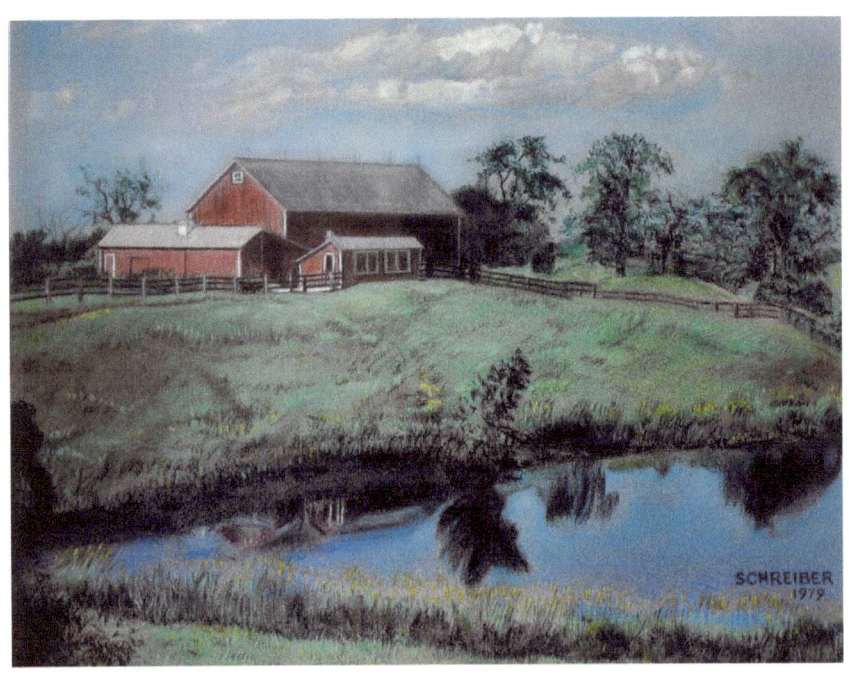

Farm House, 13" x 17" pastel

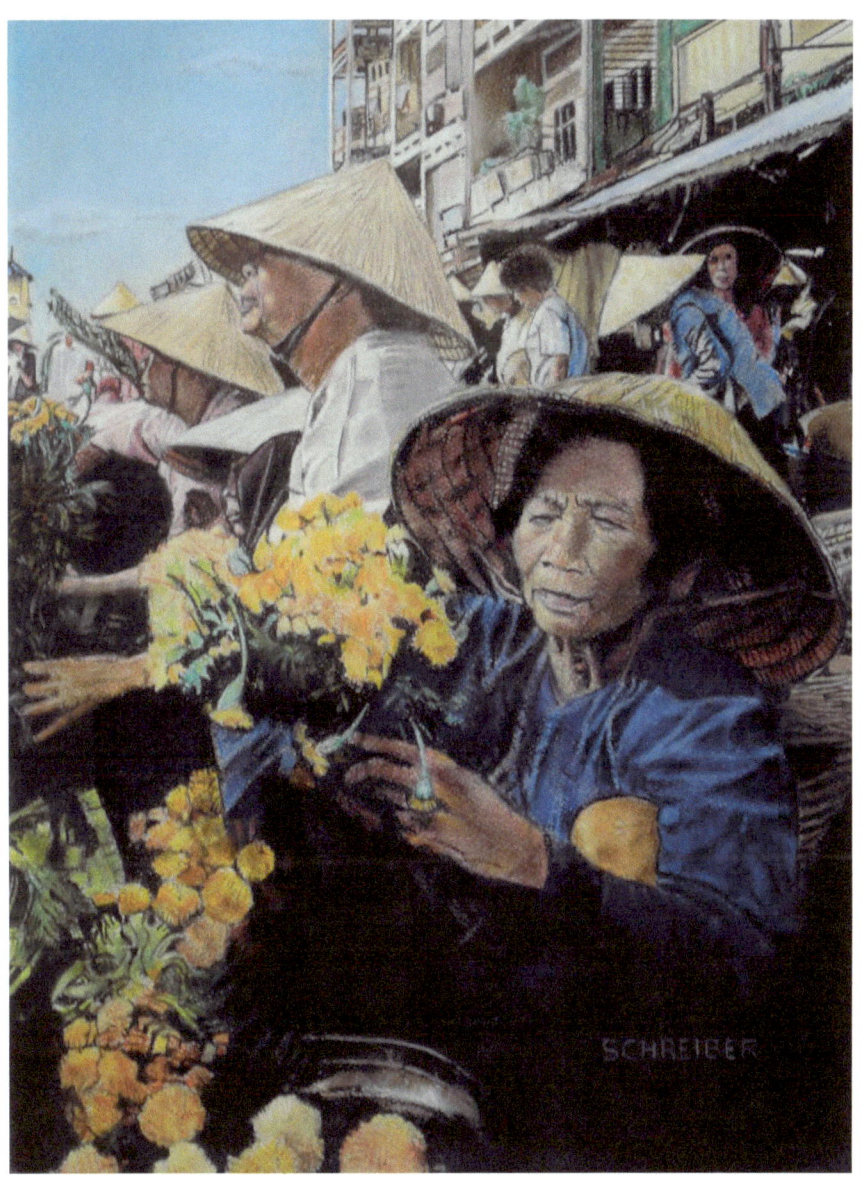

Flower Market, 12" x 16" pastel

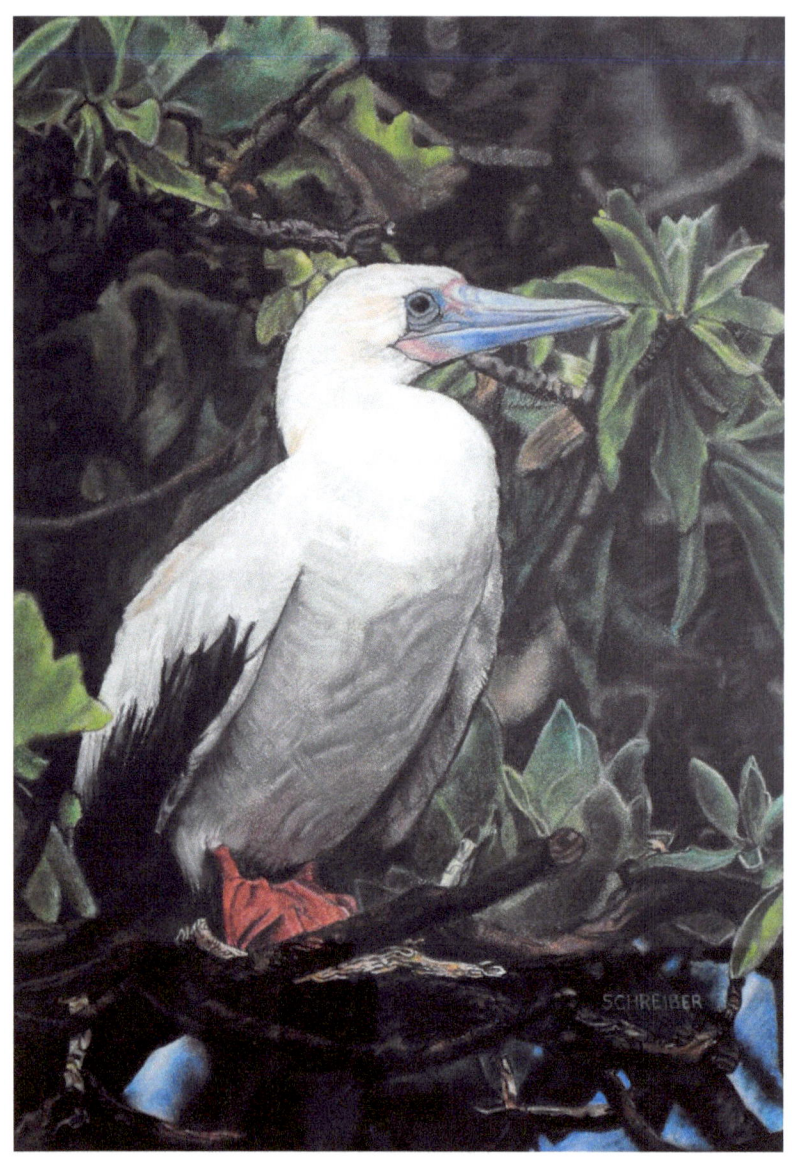

Booby, 15" x 22" pastel

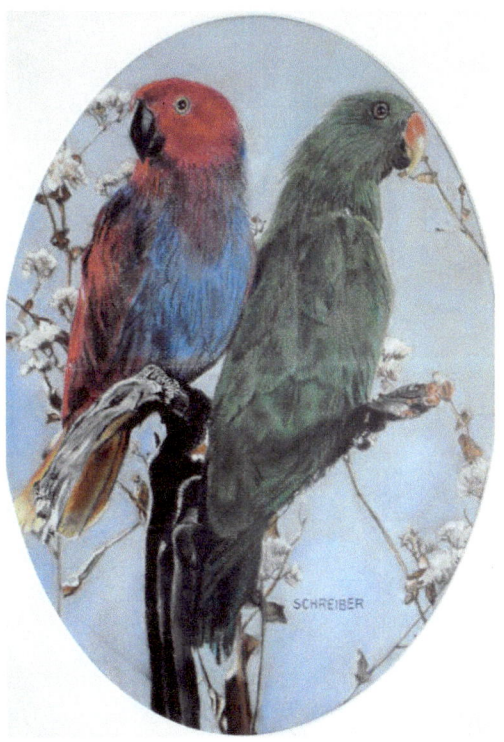

We're Not Talking
12" x 16" pastel

Red Neck Parrot
7" x 10" pastel

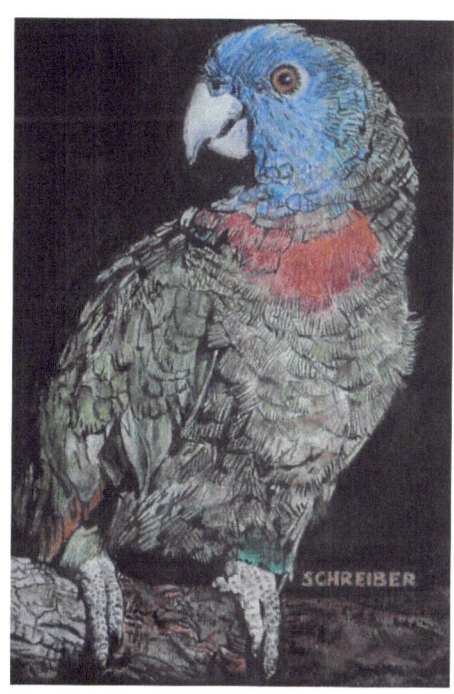

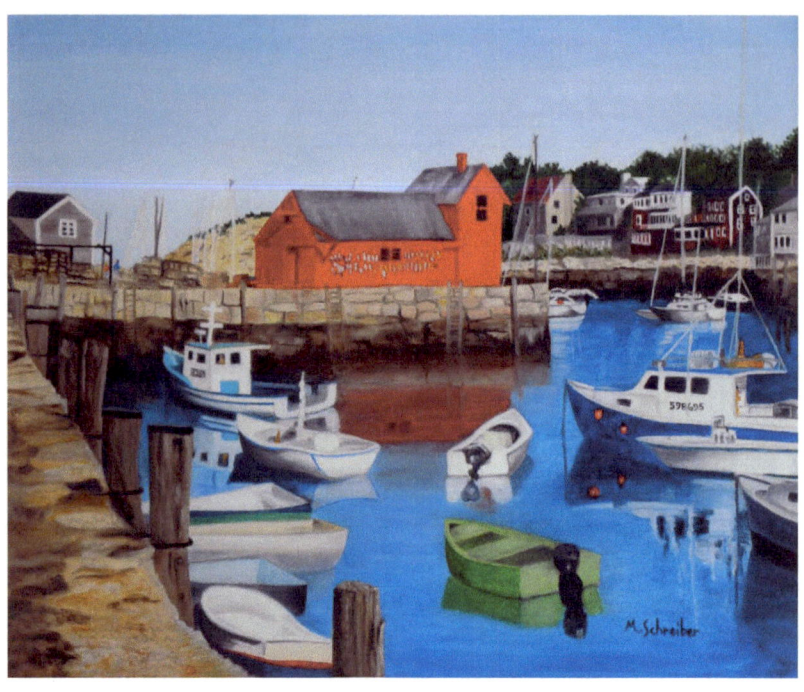

Rockport, 20" x 24" oil on canvas by M. Schreiber

THE APPLE

Though Dad loved pastels, oil paints captured me. My freshman year of college, I studied Theatre Arts at Emerson College in Boston, but the summer before my sophomore year, I bought my first oil painting kit. I took it with me when I dropped out of school to go to a kibbutz in Israel. The following year I returned to the States to study art. I received my B.A. in Fine Arts Education in 1969 from Newark State College, now Kean University, Union, New Jersey. I never intended to teach and would have preferred going to a commercial art school, but Mom and Dad wanted me to have a college education, and Dad was biased towards Fine Arts.

In my early twenties I moved to Cambridge, Massachusetts where I spent a few years trying to make it as an artist. I painted full-time, was a juried member of the Cambridge Art Association, and earned a little money teaching oil painting as an instructor for a Boston adult education program.

My painting style was flat and hard edge. Like the coloring books I enjoyed as a child, I liked painting landscapes and still life in oils using solid colors with black outlines.

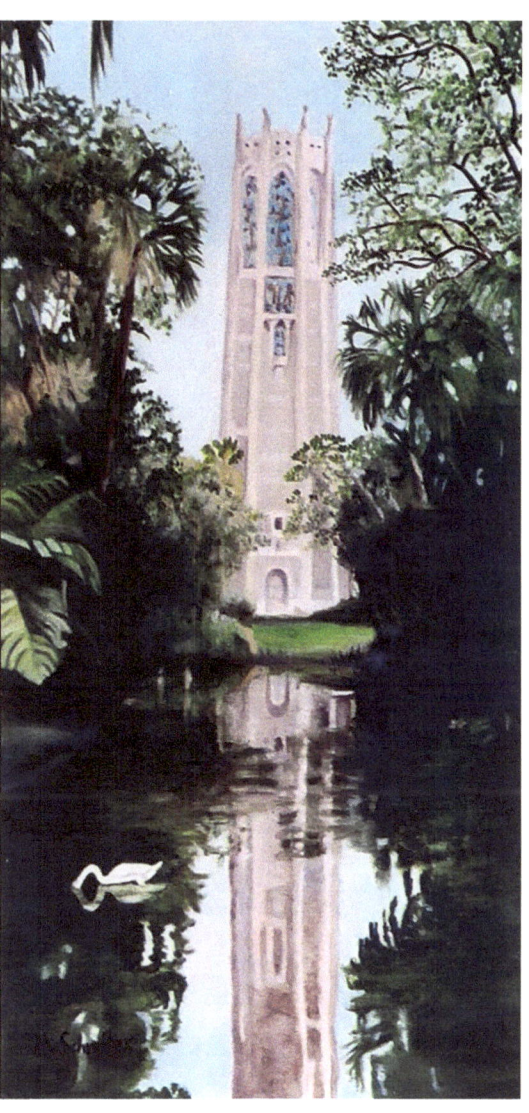

Bok Tower, 12" x 24" oil on canvas

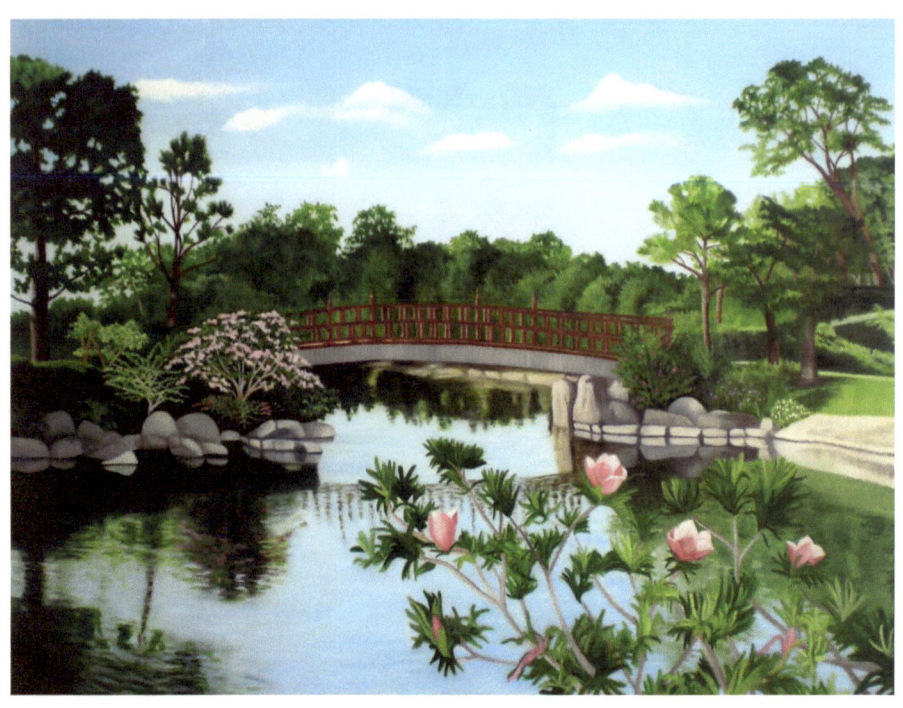

Morikami Bridge, 36" x 48" oil on canvas

I was attracted to the character in the New England arch-
tecture and painted houses and buildings in Cambridge,
Boston, and the surrounding area, all in my coloring
book style. When I acknowledged that I was "a starving
artist," I decided to return to school and in 1977
received an M.Ed. in Expressive Therapies from Lesley
University.

For over thirty years I was employed as a Mental Health
Counselor, sixteen of those years in my own private
practice in West Palm Beach, Florida. When I moved to
Florida in the early 80's, I stopped painting. The lush
vegetation and the hot climate didn't match my style or
the mood of my work, which some compared to one of
my favorite painters, Hopper. So, for over fifteen years

I didn't paint and focused on my psychotherapy career. Then in the summer of 2001, I began to see paintings everywhere in my mind's eye. I took out my easel and began to paint. I haven't stopped since.

In 2002, I was juried into Women in the Visual Arts, and in 2005 after living through three hurricanes, I decided to follow my passion. I closed my practice to paint and exhibit my work full-time. Since then my oil paintings have been in numerous juried exhibits in local museums, galleries, and Art in Public Places.

I see beauty in the world wherever I go, and I love recreating what I see by painting landscapes. The lush flora of Florida particularly inspires me, but I also enjoy illustrating my travels to other places. My goal is to express what I felt in a particular place at a moment in time. Some experiences have motivated me to paint "collage style" works, which depict several

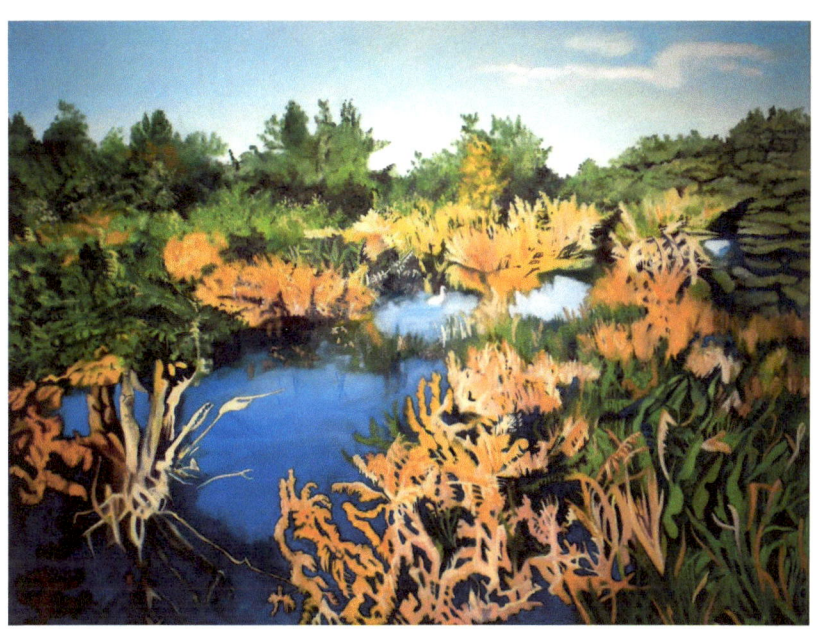

Wakodahatchee November, 30" x 40" oil on canvas

images of the same place on a single canvas.

In addition to painting, showing and selling my work, I get equal pleasure writing about the artists and establishments that make up the art community in Palm Beach County. A former columnist for *BestofArtists.com* and the *IndianRiverArtNews.com* as well as *West Palm Beach Fine Arts Examiner* for *Examiner.com*, I have published hundreds of articles to educate the public about the fabulous art scene.

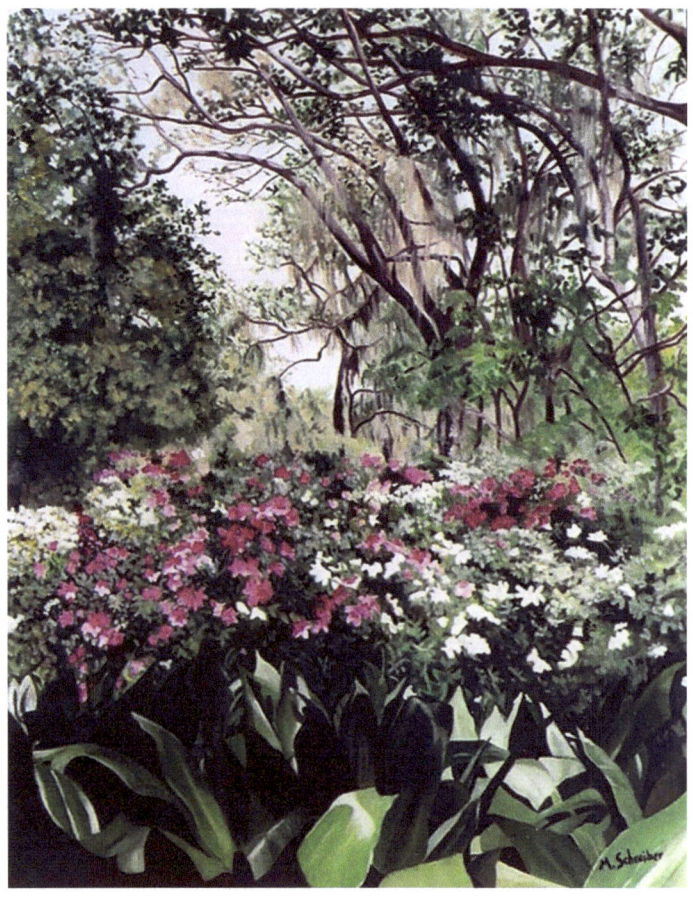

Bok Garden II, 24" x 30" oil on canvas

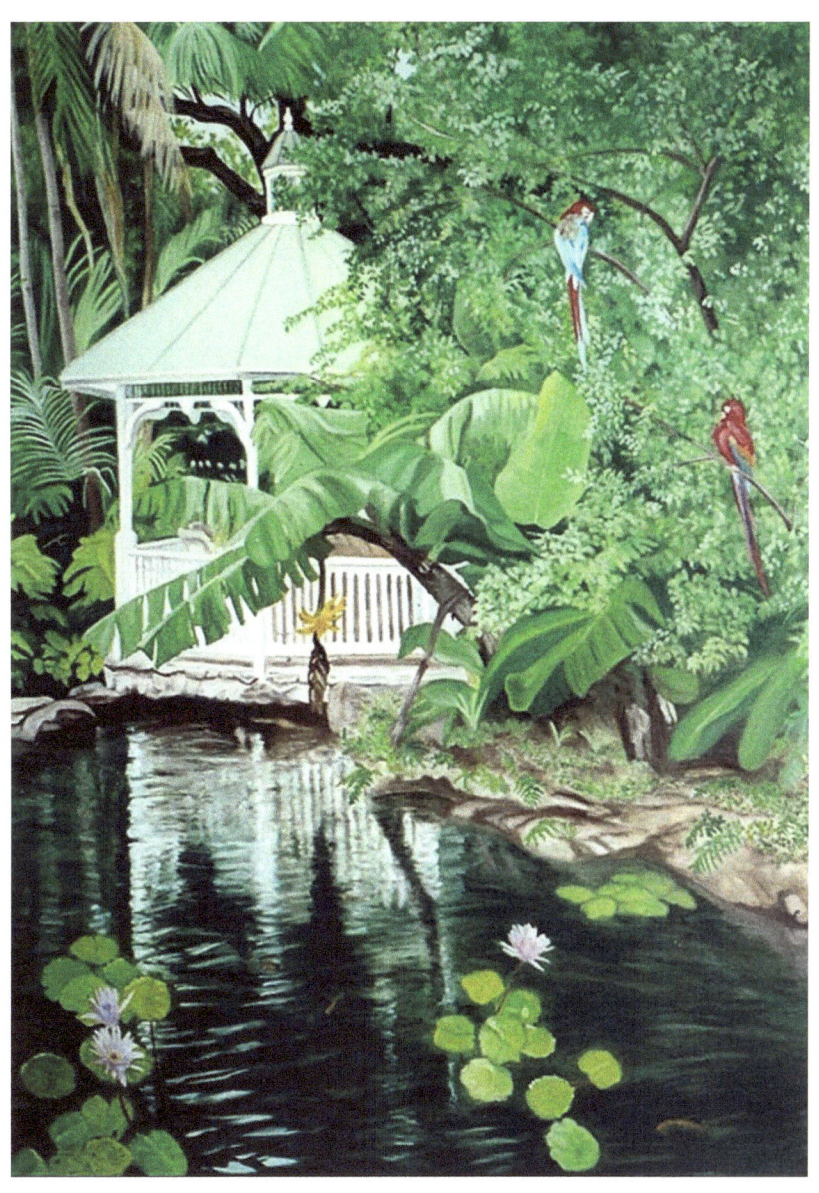

Sundy Gazebo, 36" x 48" oil on canvas

27

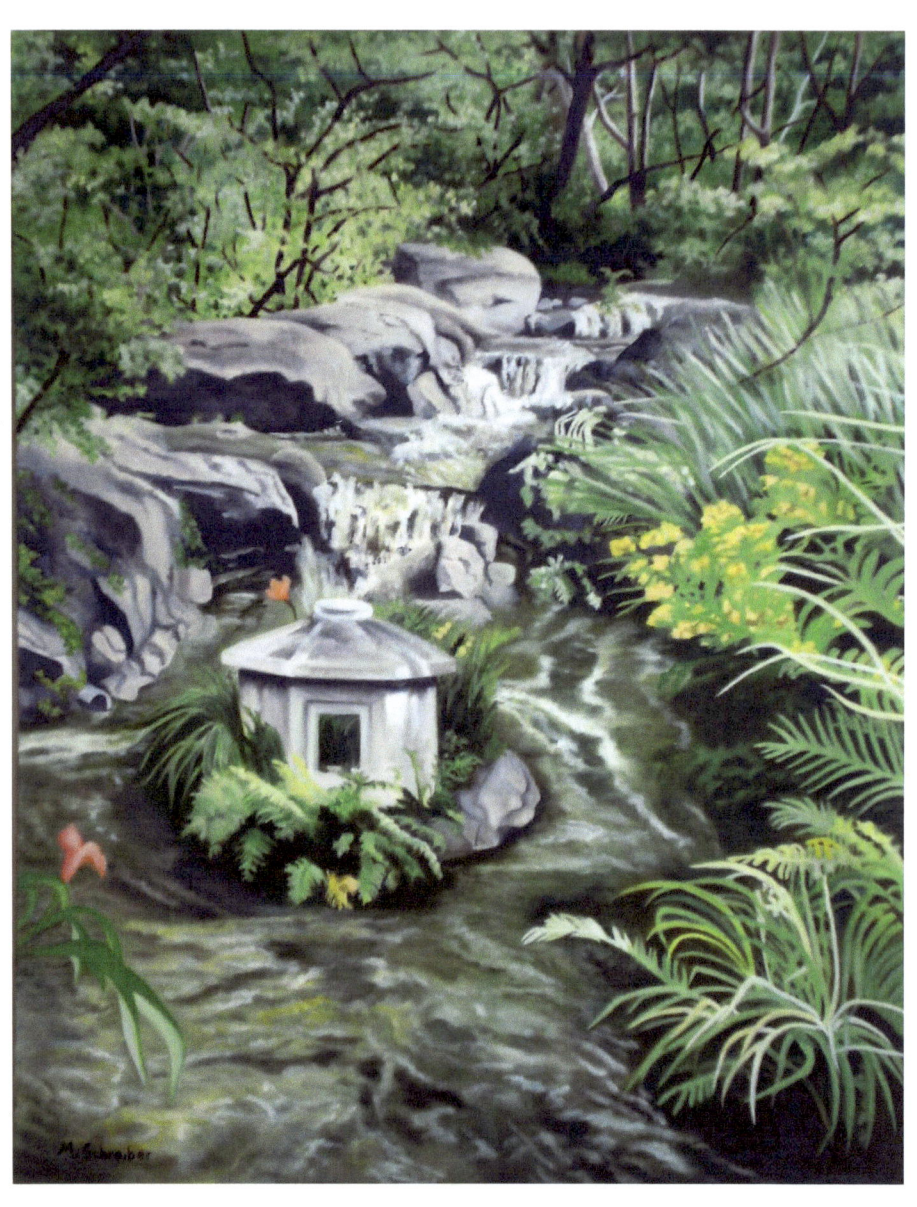

Morikami Waterfall, 24" x 30" oil on canvas

Orchids in the Entry,
16" x 20"
oil on canvas

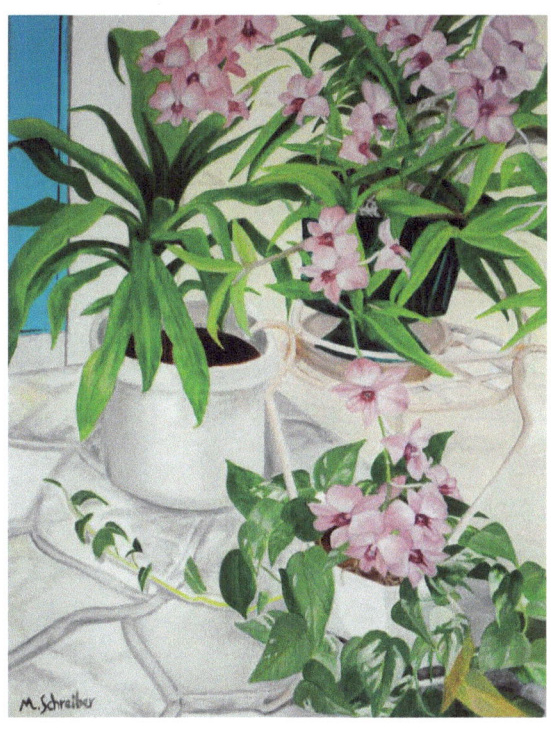

Orchid Meditation,
12" x 16" oil on canvas

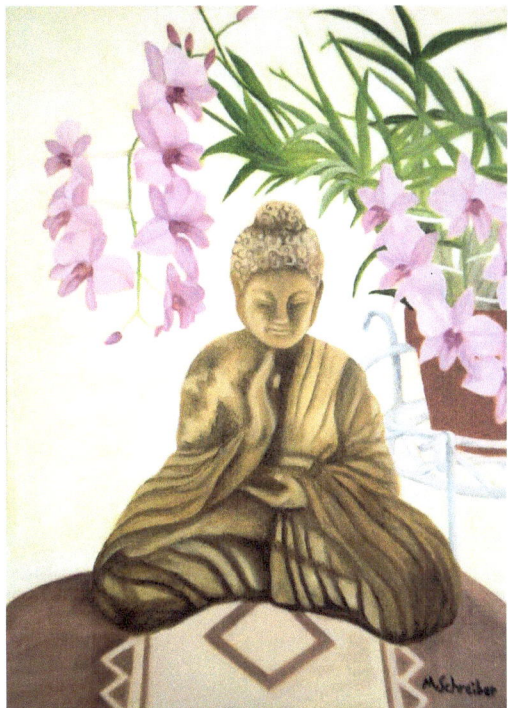

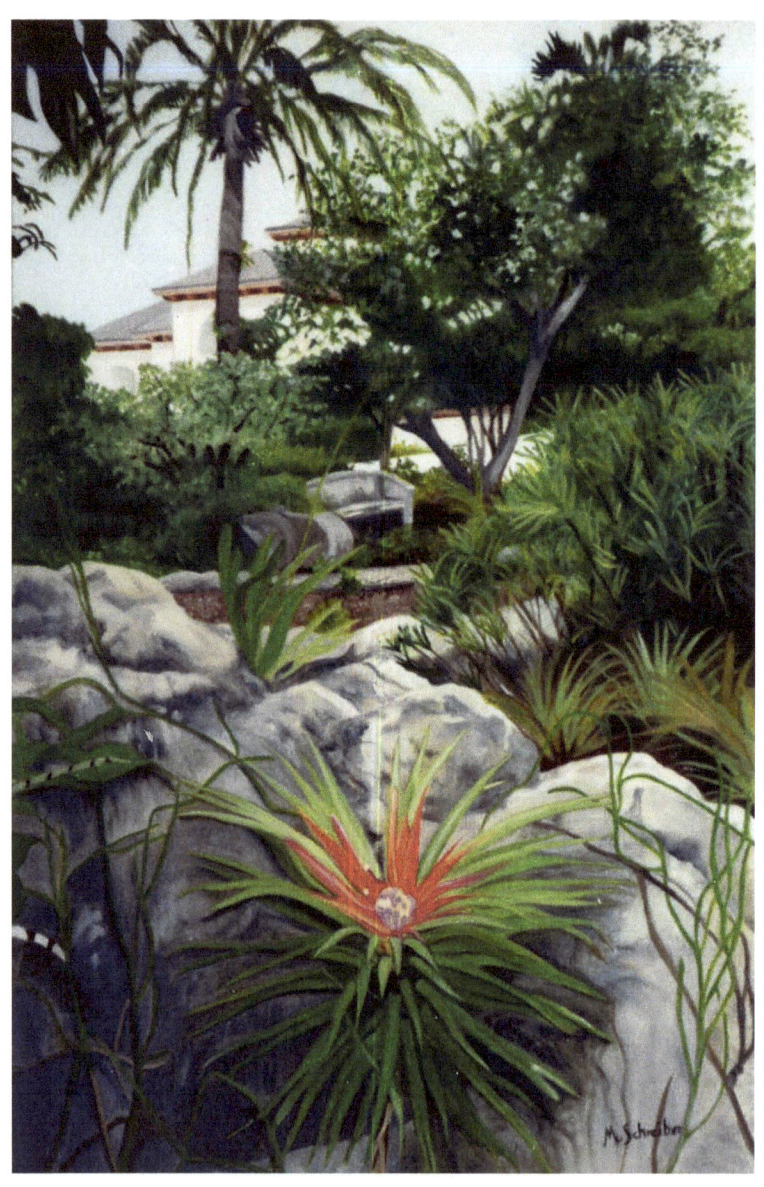

AOS Rock Garden, 20" x 30" oil on canvas

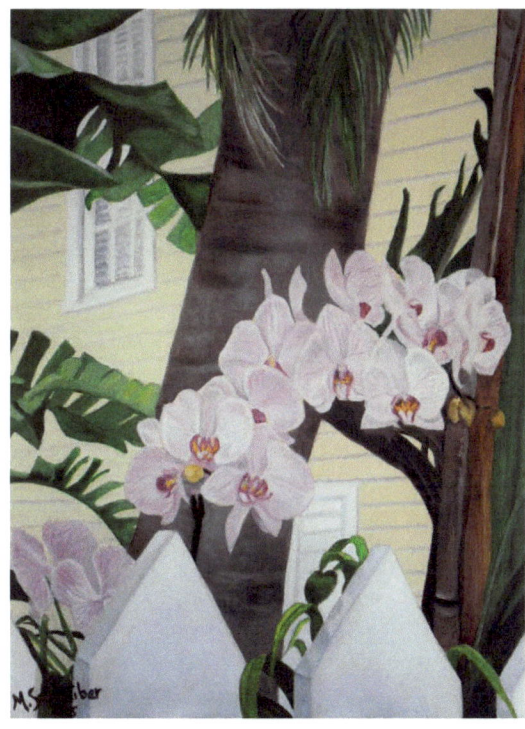

Orchids on Eaton,
12" x 16" oil on canvas

Bridge of Flowers,
16" x 20"
oil on canvas

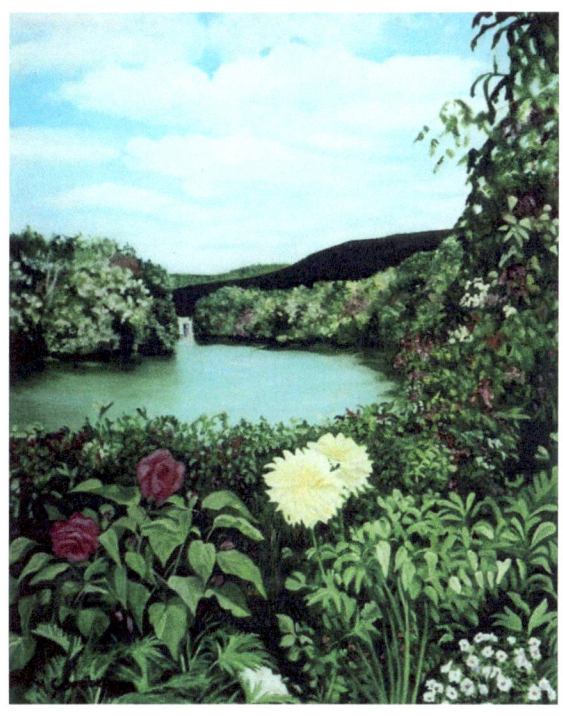

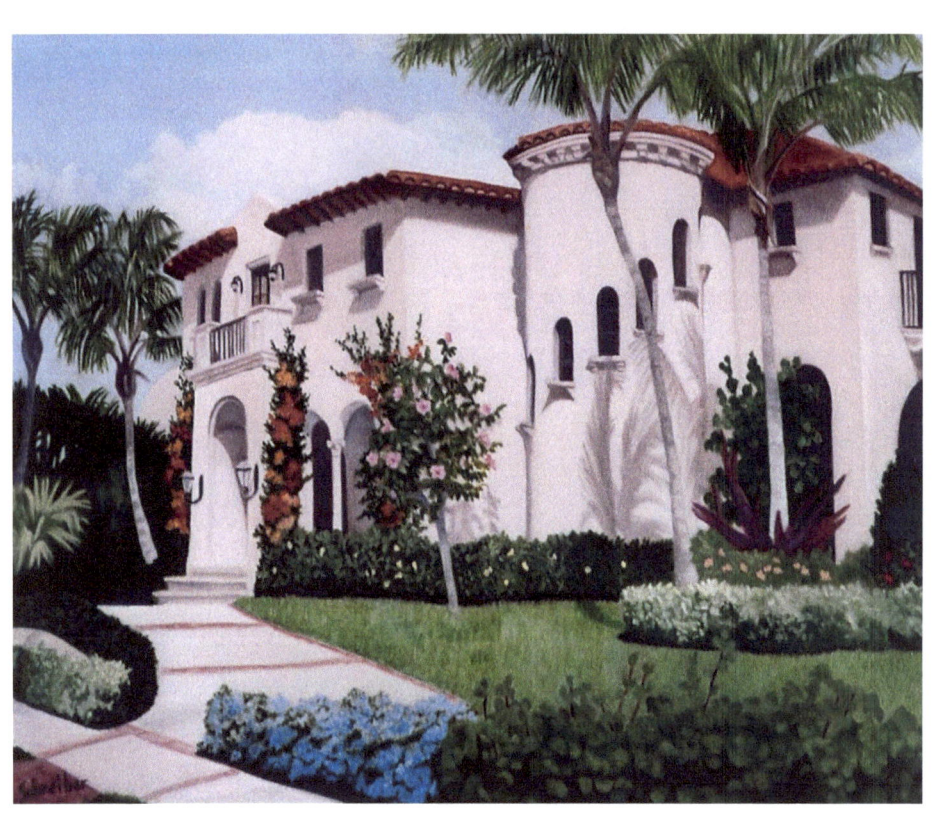

The Castle, 20" x 24" oil on canvas

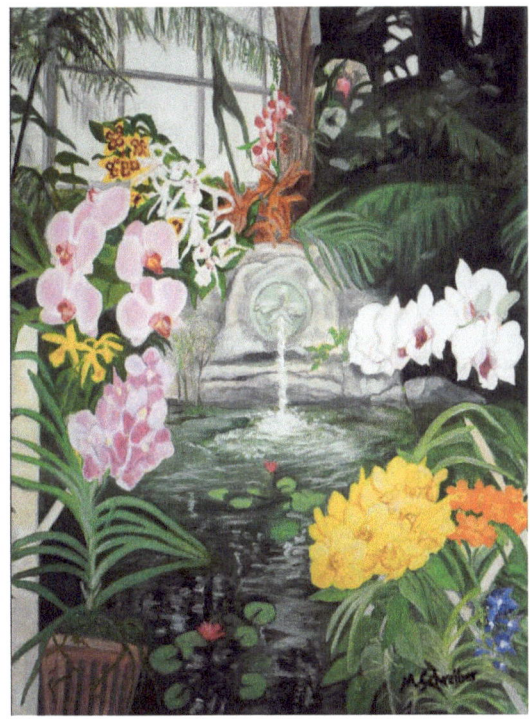

Orchid Collage,
12" x 16" oil on canvas

Experiencing
the Mango Inn
20" x 24"
oil on canvas

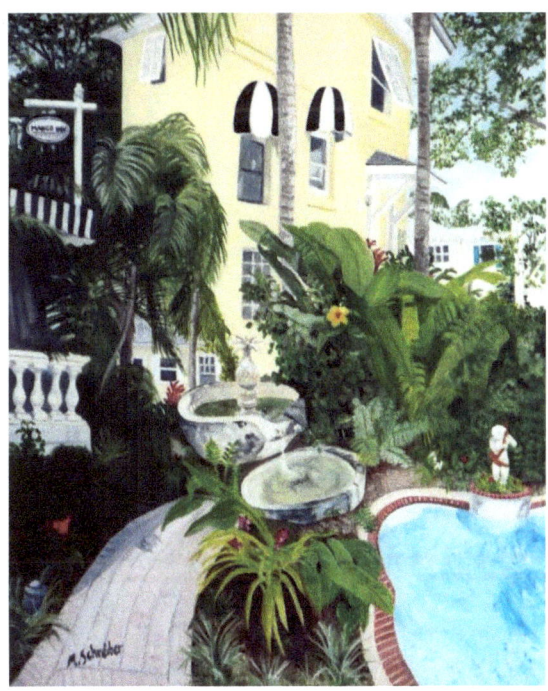

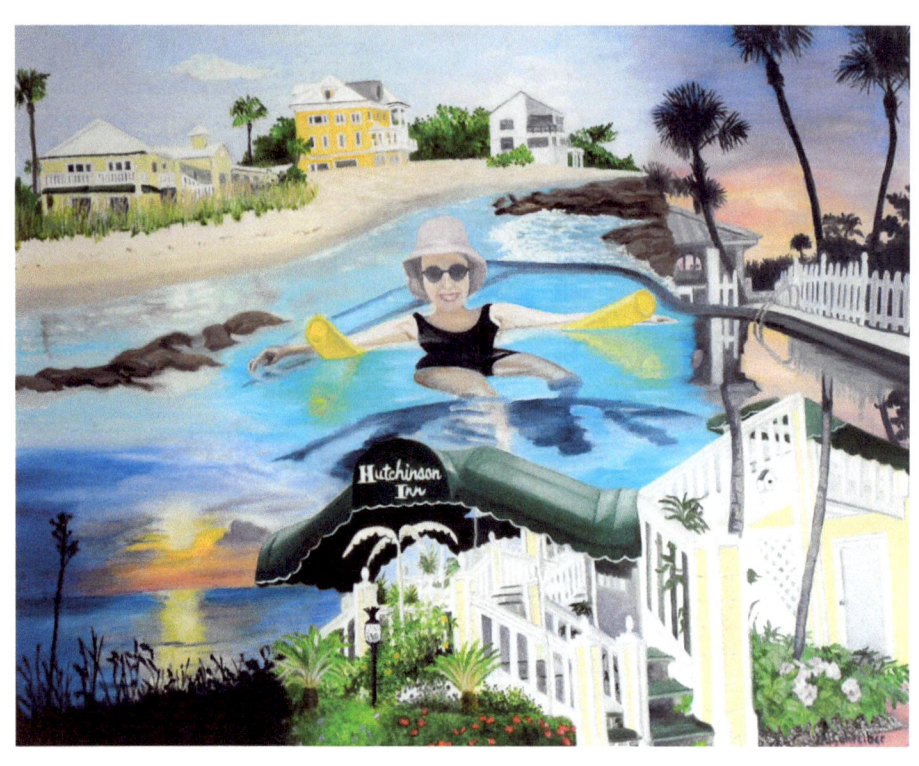

Before the Hurricanes, 22" x 28" oil on canvas

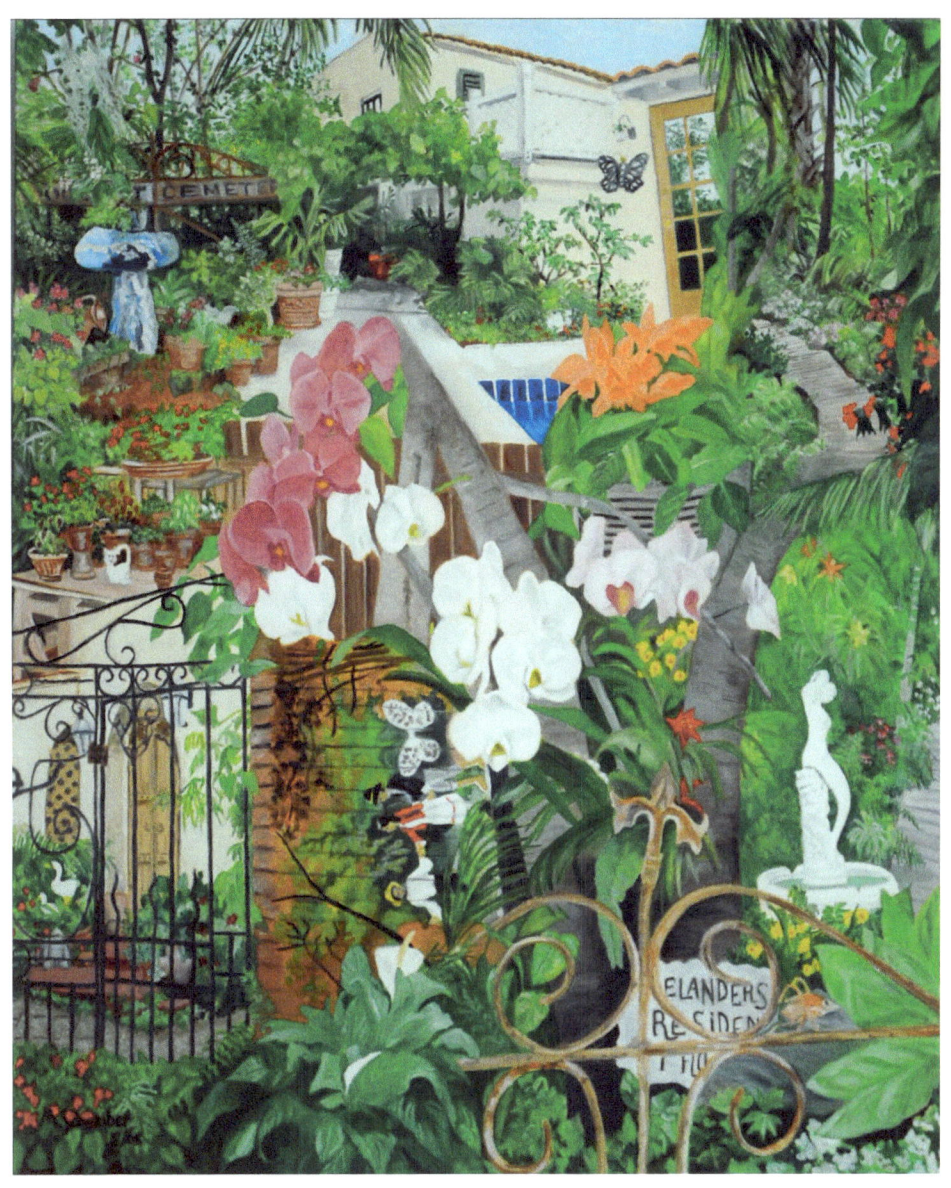

Homage to Bruce, 20" x 24" oil on canvas

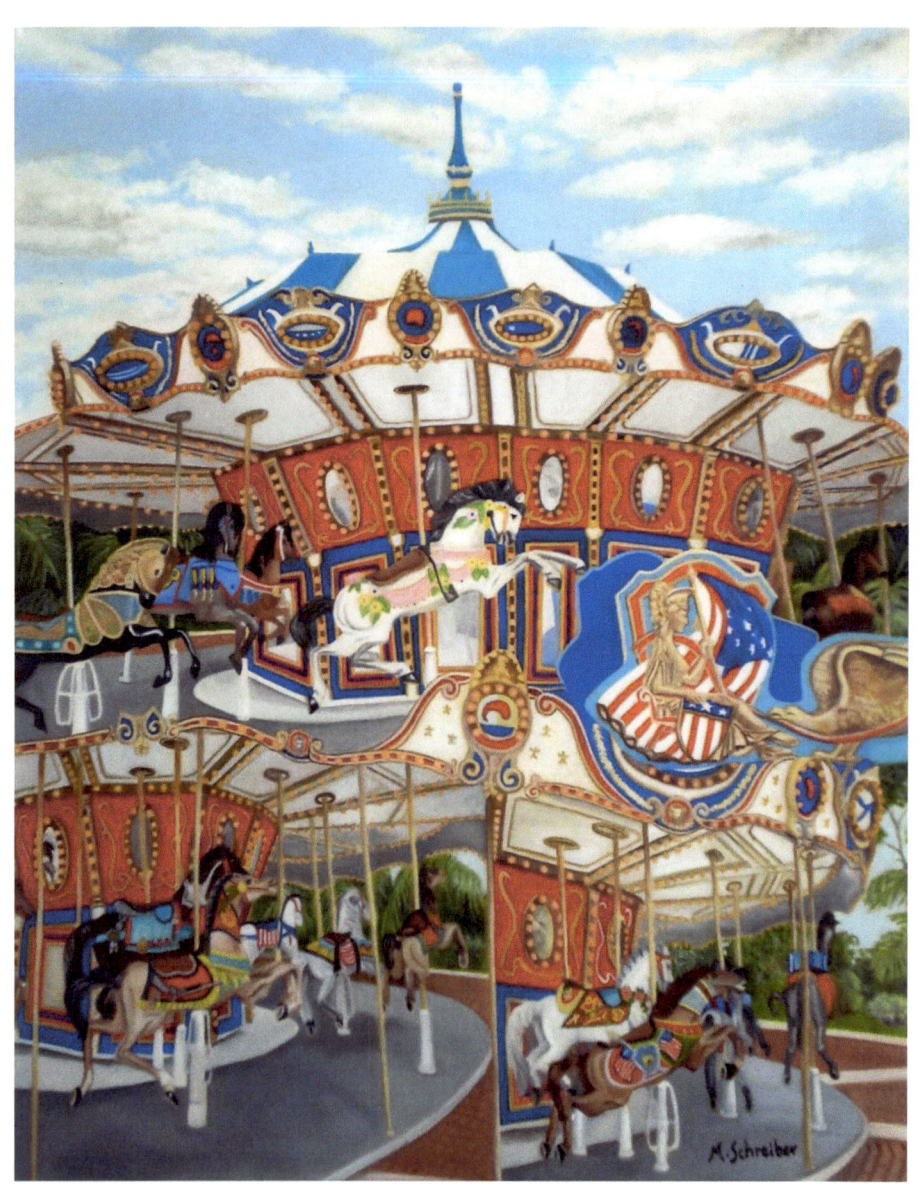

Sugar Sand Park Carousel, 24" x 30" oil on canvas

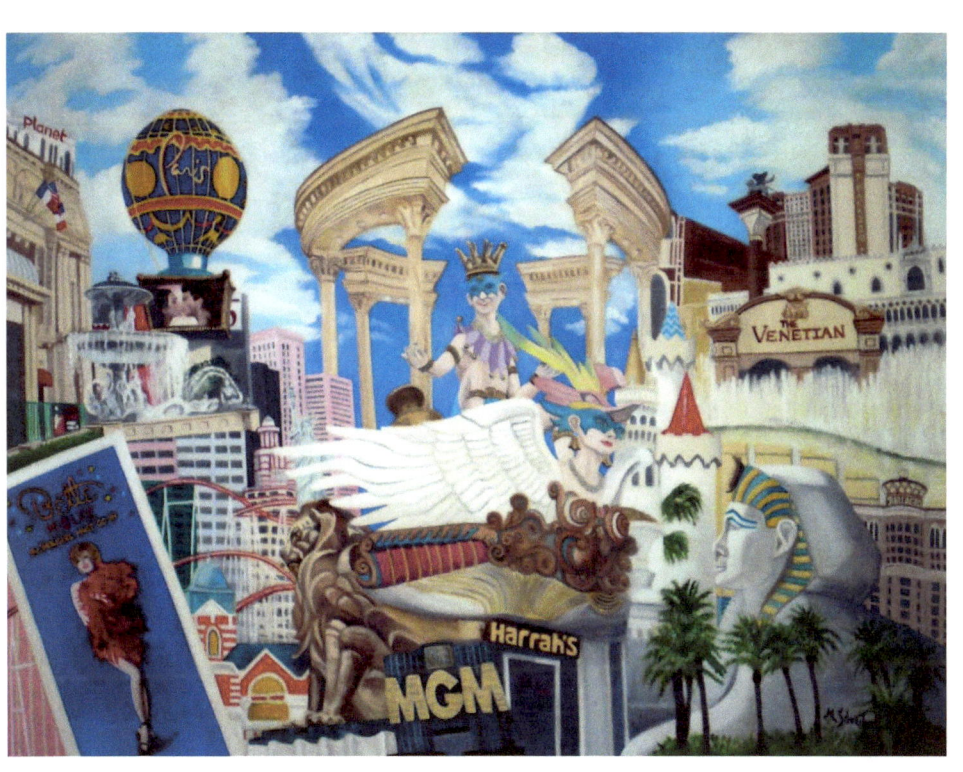

Sin City, 36"x 48" oil on canvas

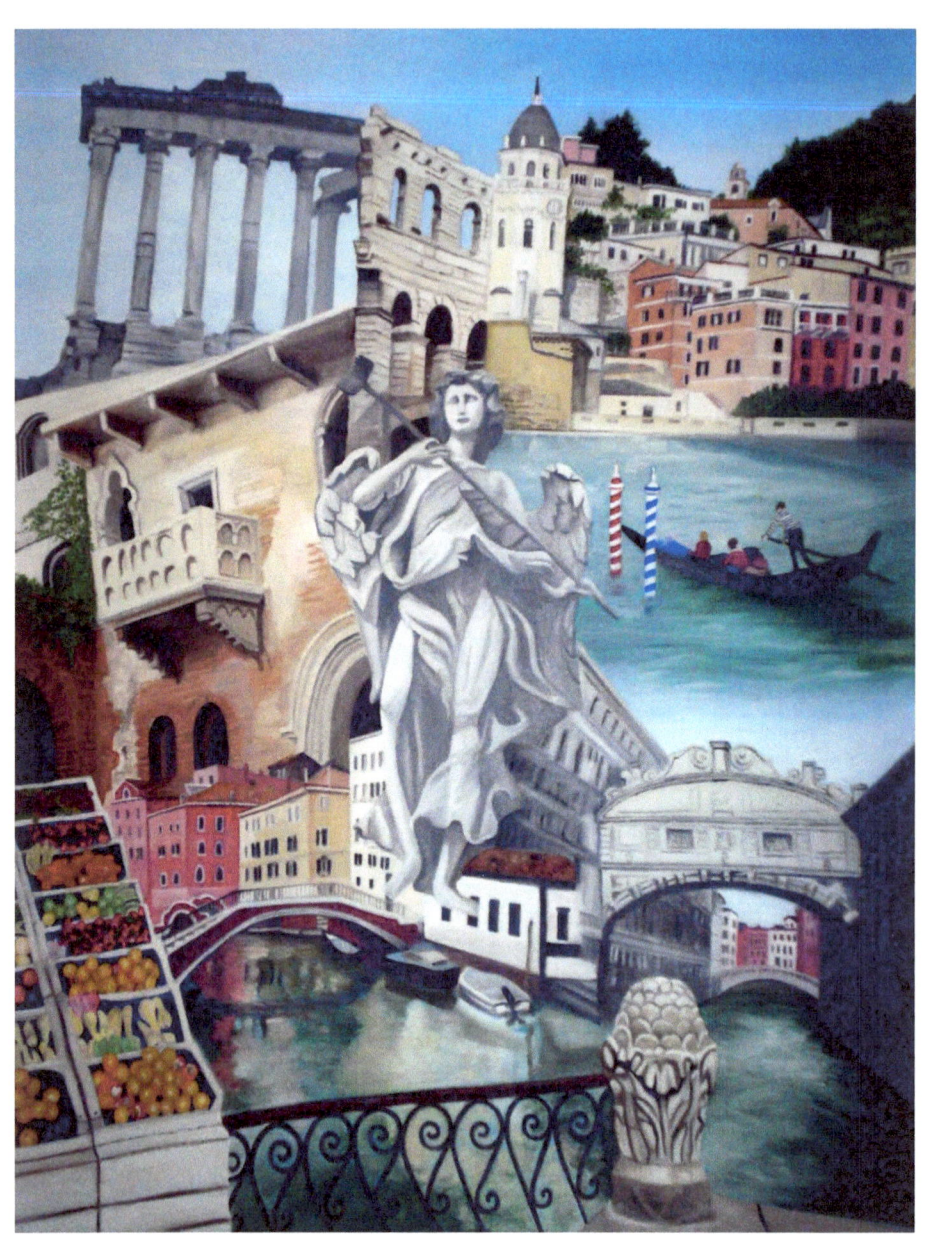

Remembering Italy, 24" x 30" oil on canvas

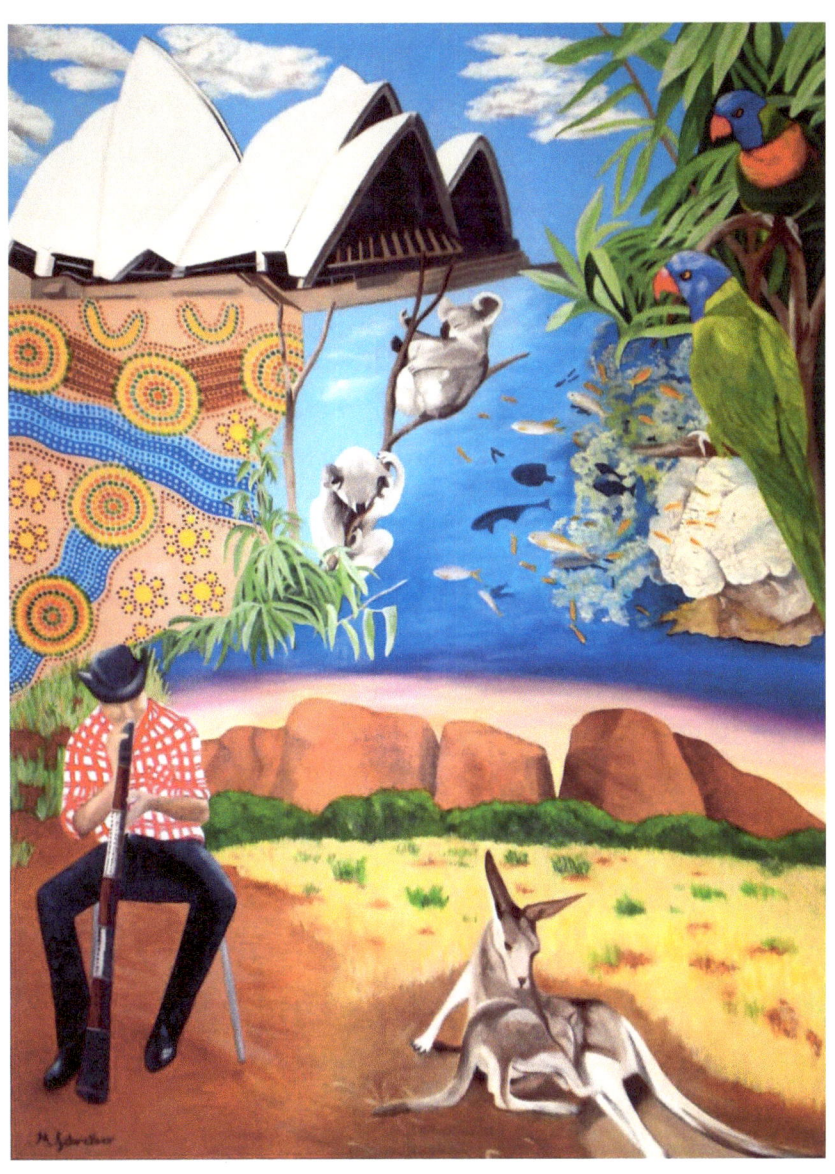

The Journey, 36" x 48" oil on canvas

GALLERIES:

Art on Park Gallery, 800 Park Avenue, Lake Park, Florida, November 2012 - present.
A Unique Art Gallery, 226 Center Street, Jupiter,Florida, June 2010 - March 2012.
Rare Earth Gallery, 41 Southwest Flagler Avenue, Stuart. Florida, February 2010 - August 2011.
Ross Gallery of Art, 2900 S. Dixie Highway, West Palm Beach, Florida, May 2010 - October 2010.
Exor Galleries, 293 Via Naranjas, Boca Raton,Florida, April 2010 - October 2010.
Urs Art Studio Gallery, 802 North Federal Highway, Boynton Beach, Florida, October 2009 - January 2010.
Aquarian Age Gallery, 2884 South Federal Hwy,Boca Raton, Florida, January - March 2008.
Beyond Decor Fine Art Gallery, 211 Royal Poinciana Way, Palm Beach, Florida, March 2006 - January 2007.
The Unknown Artist Gallery, 120 South Dixie Hwy,West Palm Beach, Florida, October 2004 - January 2006.
Pandora's Hope, 167 Northeast 2nd Avenue, DelrayBeach, Florida, February - August 2005.

AFFILIATIONS:

National Association of Women Artists & N.A.W.A. Florida Chapter, New York, NY, March 2014 - Present.
Artists of Palm Beach County, West Palm Beach, FL, January 2008 - Present.
Florida Writers Association, FL, June 2008 – Present.
Women in the Visual Arts, Inc., Boca Raton, FL, November 2002 – Present.
Artists Association of Jupiter, Jupiter, FL, June 2010 – March 2012.
Lighthouse ArtCenter, Tequesta, FL, Jan. 2010 – 2012.
Artists' Guild of the Palm Beaches, West Palm Beach, FL, 2006 - 2007.
Armory Art Center, West Palm Beach, FL, February 2005 – 2009.
Lake Worth Art League, Lake Worth, FL, 2004.
Norton Museum of Art. West Palm Beach, FL, September 1983 – Present.

www.ingramcontent.com/pod-product-compliance
Lightning Source LLC
Chambersburg PA
CBHW041142180526
45159CB00002BB/709